Pet Pleasers *for*
Dog Lovers™

Edited by Jeanne Stauffer

HOUSE of WHITE BIRCHES
PUBLISHERS
SINCE 1947

Table of Contents

*For You & Your
Pampered Pooch,
page 35*

*Home for the
Family Dog,
page 40*

*My Dog & Me,
page 28*

*Slip-Stitch Style
Dog Sweater,
page 12*

General Information

How To Determine Size

For proper fit, measure dog around chest just behind front legs. Follow instructions for this size; if chest measurement falls between sizes, follow instructions for next larger size.

Measure dog's back from just above tail to midpoint of neck. If dog is longer or shorter than specified length for desired chest size, add or subtract length while working body and before beginning leg openings.

Additional yarn may be necessary if more than 2 inches of extra length is added.

Best Friend Tote & Vest, **page 42**

Abbreviations & Symbols

approx · · · · · · approximately
beg · · · · · · · begin/beginning
CC · · · · · · · contrasting color
ch · · · · · · · · chain stitch
cm · · · · · · · centimeter(s)
cn · · · · · · · · cable needle
dec · · · · · · decrease/decreases/ decreasing
dpn(s) · · double-pointed needle(s)
g · · · · · · · · · · · · gram
inc · · increase/increases/increasing
k · · · · · · · · · · · · · · knit
k2tog · · · · knit 2 stitches together
LH · · · · · · · · · · · left hand
lp(s) · · · · · · · · · · loop(s)
m · · · · · · · · · · · meter(s)
M1 · · · · · · · make one stitch
MC · · · · · · · · · main color
mm · · · · · · · · millimeter(s)
oz · · · · · · · · · · ounce(s)
p · · · · · · · · · · · · · · purl

pat(s) · · · · · · · · · pattern(s)
p2tog · · · · purl 2 stitches together
psso · · · · · pass slipped stitch over
p2sso · · · pass 2 slipped stitches over
rem · · · · · · · · remain/remaining
rep · · · · · · · · · · · repeat(s)
rev St st · · · reverse stockinette stitch
RH · · · · · · · · · · right hand
rnd(s) · · · · · · · · · · rounds
RS · · · · · · · · · · · right side
skp · · · · slip, knit, pass stitch over— one stitch decreased
sk2p · · · · · · slip 1, knit 2 together, pass slip stitch over, then knit 2 together—2 stitches have been decreased
sl · · · · · · · · · · · · · · slip
sl 1k · · · · · · · · slip 1 knitwise
sl 1p · · · · · · · · slip 1 purlwise
sl st · · · · · · · · slip stitch(es)
ssk · · · · slip, slip, knit these 2 stitches together—a decrease

st(s) · · · · · · · · · · stitch(es)
St st · · · · · · · stockinette stitch/ stocking stitch
tbl · · · · · through back loop(s)
tog · · · · · · · · · together
WS · · · · · · · · · wrong side
wyib · · · · · · with yarn in back
wyif · · · · · · with yarn in front
yd(s) · · · · · · · · · · yard(s)
yfwd · · · · · · · yarn forward
yo · · · · · · · · · · yarn over

[ ] work instructions within brackets as many times as directed
( ) work instructions within parentheses in the place directed
** repeat instructions following the asterisks as directed
* repeat instructions following the single asterisk as directed
" inch(es)

House of White Birches, Berne, Indiana 46711   DRGnetwork.com

Laddie Dog Sweater

Design by Laura Polley

Skill Level

■■■□ INTERMEDIATE

Sizes

Small (medium, large, extra-large) Instructions are given for smallest size, with larger sizes in parentheses. When only 1 number is given, it applies to all sizes. To determine size see General Information on page 3.

Finished Measurements

Chest: 12½ (15½, 19½, 25) inches
Back: 12 (14½, 19, 20) inches, excluding fringe

Materials

- Worsted weight yarn: 3½ (5, 7, 8) oz black (A); 3 oz each red (B) and white (C)
- Size 9 (5.25mm) 24-inch long circular needle or size needed to obtain gauge
- Size H/8 (5mm) crochet hook
- Stitch holder
- 2 split stitch markers
- Yarn needle

Gauge

16 sts = 4 inches/10cm in St st.
To save time, take time to check gauge.

Special Abbreviations

Make 1 (M1): Insert tip of LH needle from front to back under horizontal thread between st just worked and next st, k1-tbl.
Increase (inc): Increase 1 st by knitting in front and back of next st.

Stripe Sequence

Work the following color sequence in pat as established knitting the knit sts and purling the purl sts:

*10 rows A,
2 rows C,
4 rows A,
2 rows B.
Rep from * for pat.

Pattern Notes

Circular needle used to accommodate stitches. Do not join; work back and forth in rows.

When changing colors at end of row, drop A (do not cut), pick up again when needed; cut off B and C at end of each two-row section.

When working from chart, odd-numbered rows are wrong side rows and are worked from left to right; even-numbered rows are right side rows and are worked from right to left.

Work Make 1 increases one stitch in from the edge.

Back

With A, cast on 20 (22, 32, 50) sts.

Set up pat

Row 1 (WS): P1 (2, 7, 2), k1, p2, k1, [p10, k1, p2, k1] 1 (1, 1, 3) time(s), p1 (2, 7, 2).

Rows 2 (RS)–30 (33, 37, 35): Working in pat as established, follow Laddie Dog Sweater Chart working M1 in as indicated 1 st in from each edge—32 (38, 50, 64) sts.

Mark each end of last row for side seams.

Continue in pat and Color Sequence as established until piece measures 8 (9¼, 11, 13) from cast-on edge.

For leg opening: Continue in pat, bind off 5 (5, 6, 6) sts at beg of next 2 rows—22 (28, 38, 52) sts.

Continue in pat and color sequence until piece

measures 9 (11, 13, 16) inches from cast-on edge, ending with WS row.

Neck Band

Row 1 (RS): On first side, work in pat across first 8 (10, 14, 17) sts; place next 6 (8, 10, 18) sts on holder for neck; on 2nd side, join 2nd skein yarn and work in pat across rem 8 (10, 14, 17) sts.

Row 2: Working both sides at once with separate skeins, work in pat across first side; on 2nd side, bind off 1 (2, 2, 2) st(s), work in pat across rem sts.

Row 3: Work in pat across first side; on 2nd side, bind off 1 (2, 2, 2) st(s), work in pat across rem sts—7 (8, 12, 15) sts on each side.

Rows 4–6: Work in pat across both sides.

Row 7: Work in pat across first side to last 2 sts, k2tog; on 2nd side, k2tog, work in pat across—6 (7, 11, 14) sts on each side.

Rep [Rows 4–7] 1 (2, 2, 3) times—5 (5, 9, 11) sts on each side.

Work even in pat across each side until piece measures 12 (15, 18, 22) inches from cast-on edge.

Bind off each side.

Vertical Plaid Lines

Note: Vertical rows are worked over purl sts columns on RS of work.

To work each Plaid Line: With RS side facing, holding yarn behind work, insert crochet hook from front to back through first st at bottom of purl st column, pull loop of yarn through to front, *move up to next row and insert hook into next purl st on column, pull loop of yarn through st to front and through loop on hook; rep from * to top of column. Cut yarn and pull end through loop on hook.

House of White Birches, Berne, Indiana 46711   DRGnetwork.com

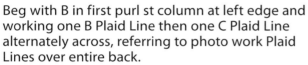

Beg with B in first purl st column at left edge and working one B Plaid Line then one C Plaid Line alternately across, referring to photo work Plaid Lines over entire back.

Collar

With A and RS of neck band facing, beg at bind-off on one side and ending at bind-off on other side, pick up and knit 17 (17, 22, 22) sts evenly spaced in ends of rows across neck edge to center front holder, knit 6 (8, 10, 18) sts from holder, pick up and knit 17 (17, 22, 22) evenly spaced in ends of rows across to bind-off—40 (42, 54, 62) sts.

Knit 3 rows.

Bind off purlwise loosely.

With A, sew bound-off sts on first and 2nd sides of neck band tog; sew ends of rows on collar tog.

Front

On opposite ends of rows on neck band, measure and mark 1 (1½, 2, 3) inches on each side of center front neck band seam.

With A and RS of neck band facing, pick up and knit 9 (13, 17, 25) sts evenly spaced between markers.

Work in St st until front measures 2½ (3, 3½, 4) inches from neck band.

For leg opening: Knit across next 2 rows, casting on 5 (5, 6, 6) sts at end of each row—19 (23, 29, 37) sts.

Work in St st until piece measures same as back from leg opening to marked row on back, ending with WS row.

Bind off loosely.

Right Leg Band and Side Seam

With A and RS of right leg opening facing, beg in first bind-off st on back and ending in last cast-on st on front, pick up and knit 30 (34, 38, 42) sts evenly spaced around entire leg opening.

Knit 1 row.

Bind off purlwise loosely; cut yarn leaving end for sewing.

With RS tog and allowing 1 st on each end for seam, sew ends of rows on leg band tog. Matching bind-off sts on front to marked row on back, sew ends of rows on front and back tog along side.

Left Leg Band and Side Seam

Beg in last cast-on st on front and ending in first bind-off st on back, work same as right leg band; do not sew left side seam.

Bottom Band

With A and RS facing, beg in end of row below marked row on back, pick up and knit 22 (24, 26, 26) sts evenly spaced in ends of rows to cast-on; pick up and knit in 20 (22, 32, 50) cast-on sts on back, pick up and knit 22 (24, 26, 26) sts evenly spaced in ends of rows to side seam, pick up and knit in 19 (23, 29, 37) bind-off sts on front—83 (93, 113, 139) sts.

Knit 1 row.

Bind off purlwise loosely; cut yarn leaving end for sewing.

With RS tog, sew ends of rows on bottom band. Sew ends of rows on front and back tog to leg opening.

Fringe

For each knot, cut 3-inch strand each of A, B and C. Holding all 3 strands tog as one, fold in half, insert crochet hook from wrong to right side through st, pull fold through st, place yarn ends through fold and pull to tighten.

Make additional knots 1 inch apart along bottom band and each leg band. ❖

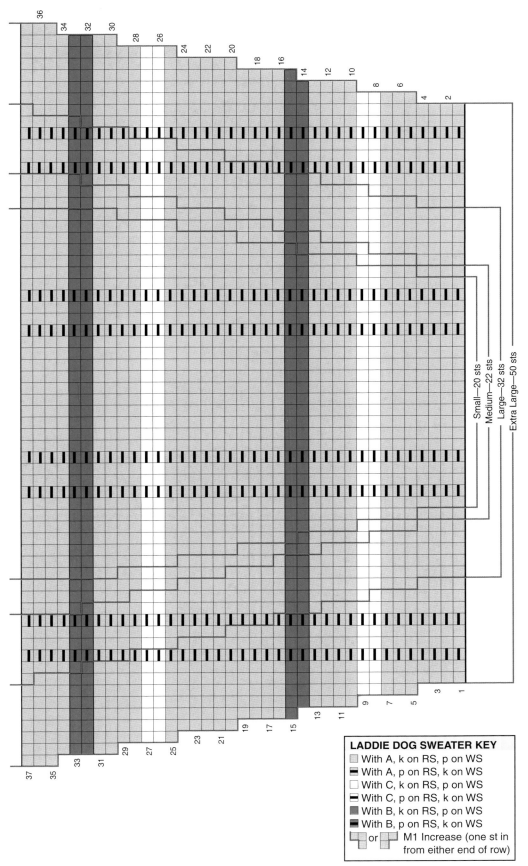

Laddie Dog Sweater Chart

Small—20 sts
Medium—22 sts
Large—32 sts
Extra Large—50 sts

LADDIE DOG SWEATER KEY

- With A, k on RS, p on WS
- With A, p on RS, k on WS
- With C, k on RS, p on WS
- With C, p on RS, k on WS
- With B, k on RS, p on WS
- With B, p on RS, k on WS
- or M1 Increase (one st in from either end of row)

House of White Birches, Berne, Indiana 46711   DRGnetwork.com

Princess Dog Sweater

Design by Laura Polley

Skill Level
■■□□ EASY

Sizes
Small (medium, large, extra-large) Instructions are given for smallest size, with larger sizes in parentheses. When only 1 size is given, it applies to all sizes. To determine size see General Information on page 3.

Finished Measurements
Chest: 13½ (15½, 20, 26½) inches around
Back: 13 (15, 19, 22) inches long

Materials

- Worsted weight yarn: 3½ (5, 7, 8) oz each dark pink (A) and white (B) and 2 (2, 3, 3) oz light pink (C)
- Size 7 (4.5mm) straight needles
- Size 9 (5.25mm) 24-inch circular needles or size needed to obtain gauge
- Stitch holder
- 2 split stitch markers
- Yarn needle

Gauge
15 sts = 4 inches/10 cm in St st with larger needles. To save time, take time to check gauge.

Special Abbreviations
Reverse stockinette stitch (rev St st): Purl sts on RS of work; knit sts on WS of work.
Make 1 (M1): Insert tip of LH needle from front to back under horizontal thread between st just worked and next st, k1-tbl.
Increase (inc): Increase 1 st by knitting in front and back of next st.

Pattern Notes
Circular needle is used to accommodate stitches. Do not join, work back and forth in rows.

Back
With larger needles and A, cast on 20 (20, 32, 48) sts.

Rows 1 and 2: Knit across.

Row 3 (RS): K1, M1, knit to last 2 sts, M1, k1—22 (22, 34, 50) sts.

Rows 4–6: Work even in St st.

Rep [Rows 3–6] 5 (7, 7, 7) times—32 (36, 48, 64) sts. Mark each end of last row for side seams.

Knit 2 rows for ridge at base of ruffle.

Work even in St st until piece measures 7½ (9, 13, 15½) inches from cast-on edge, ending with WS row.

For leg opening: Bind off 5 sts at beg of next 2 rows—22 (26, 38, 54) sts.

Work even in St st until piece measures 9 (11, 16, 19½) from cast-on edge, ending with WS row.

Neck Band
Row 1 (RS): Work in St st across first 8 (10, 14, 18) sts; place next 6 (6, 10, 18) sts on holder for neck; join 2nd skein and work in St st across rem 8 (10, 14, 18) sts.

Row 2: Purl across first side; on 2nd side, bind off 1 (1, 2, 2) sts, purl rem sts.

Row 3: Knit across first side; on 2nd side bind off 1 (1, 2, 2) sts, knit rem sts—7 (9, 12, 16) sts on each side.

Rows 4–6: Work in St st across each side.

Row 7: Knit across first side to last 2 sts, k2tog; on 2nd side, k2tog, knit rem sts—6 (8, 11, 15) sts on each side.

Rep [Rows 4–7] 1 (3, 2, 2) times—5 (5, 9, 13) sts on each side.

Work even in St st across each side until piece measures 12 (14, 17½, 20½) inches from cast-on edge.

Bind off each side.

Collar

Row 1 (RS): With smaller needles and C, with RS of neck band facing and beg at bind-off on one side and ending at bind-off on other side, pick up and knit 17 (18, 19, 19) sts evenly spaced in ends of rows across neck edge to center front holder, knit next 6 (6, 10, 18) sts from holder, pick up and knit 17 (18, 19, 19) sts evenly spaced in ends of rows across to bind-off—40 (42, 48, 56) sts.

Row 2: Purl across.

Rows 3–6: Work in St st. At end of last row, cut C.

Row 7: With B, knit inc in each st across—80 (84, 96, 112) sts.

Rows 8–16 (16, 20, 20): Beg with knit row, work in rev St st. At end of last row, cut B.

Next row: With B, *k2tog, k2; rep from * across.

Next row: Knit across.

House of White Birches, Berne, Indiana 46711   DRGnetwork.com

Bind off.

With matching colors, sew bind-off sts on first and 2nd sides of neck band tog, sew ends of rows on collar together.

Front
On opposite ends of rows on neck band, measure and mark 1 (1½, 2, 3) inches on each side of center front neck band seam.

With larger needles and A, with RS of neck band facing, pick up and knit 9 (13, 17, 25) sts evenly spaced between markers.

Work in St st until front measures 2½ (3, 3½, 4) inches from neck band.

For leg opening: Knit next 2 rows, casting on 5 sts at end of each row—19 (23, 27, 35) sts.

Work in St st until piece measures same as back from neck band to ridge, ending with RS row.

Knit 2 rows.

Bind off loosely.

Right Leg Band and Side Seam
With smaller needles and A, with RS of right leg opening facing, beg in first bind-off st on back and ending in last cast-on st on front, pick up and knit 30 (38, 42, 46) sts evenly spaced around entire leg opening.

Knit 1 row.

Bind off knitwise; cut yarn leaving end for sewing.

Allowing 1 st at each end of row for seam, with RS tog, sew ends of rows on leg band. Matching bind-off on front to marked row on back, sew ends of rows on front and back tog along side.

Left Leg Band and Side Seam
Beg in last cast-on st on front and ending in first bind-off st on back, work same as right leg band; do not sew left side seam.

Body Ruffle
Note: To pick up sts for body and tail ruffle, hold C on WS of work; from RS of work, insert needle between sts of back or front, yo with C and pull st through to RS of work.

Row 1 (RS): With smaller needles and C, holding piece with tail end toward you and head end away from you, with RS of back facing, pick up a st in each st across marked row on back, pick up a st in seam, pick up a st in each bind-off st on front—50 (58, 74, 98) sts.

Rows 2 and 3: Knit across. At end of last row, cut C.

Row 4: With B, knit across.

Row 5: Knit inc in each st across—100 (116, 148, 196) sts.

Rows 6–12: Beg with knit row, work in rev St st. At end of last row, cut B.

Row 13: With C, *k2, k2tog; rep from * across—75 (87, 111, 147) sts.

Row 14: Knit across.

Bind off.

Allowing 1 st at each end of row for seam, with RS tog, sew ends of rows on leg band. Matching bind-off on front to marked row on back, sew ends of rows on front and back tog. With matching colors, sew ends of rows on body ruffle tog.

Tail Ruffle

Row 1: With smaller needles and C, with RS of back facing, beg at left side seam, pick up and knit 18 (18, 21, 22) sts evenly spaced in ends of rows from seam to cast-on edge, pick up a st in 18 (18, 30, 46) cast-on sts, pick up and knit 18 (18, 21, 22) sts evenly spaced in ends of rows to other side seam—54 (54, 72, 90) sts.

Rows 2 and 3: Knit across. At end of last row, cut C.

Row 4: With B, knit across.

Row 5: Knit, inc in each st across—108 (108, 144, 180) sts.

Rows 6–12: Beg with knit row, work in rev St st. At end of last row, cut B.

Row 13: With C, *k2, k2tog; rep from * across—81 (81, 108, 135) sts.

Row 14: Knit across.

Bind off.

With matching colors, sew bind-off sts on first and 2nd sides of neck band tog, sew ends of rows on collar tog.

On each side, taking care not to stretch or gather either piece, sew ends of rows on tail ruffle to bind-off sts on front. ❖

Slip-Stitch Style Dog Sweater

Design by Laura Polley

Skill Level

■■■□ INTERMEDIATE

Sizes

Small (medium, large, extra-large) Instructions given for smallest size, with changes for larger sizes in parentheses. When only 1 size is given, it applies to all sizes. To determine size see General Information, page 3.

Finished Measurements

Chest: 12½ (15, 20, 26) inches
Back: 12 (14, 18, 21) inches long

Materials

- Worsted weight yarn: 3½ (7, 7, 10½) oz navy (A), 3½ oz each natural (B) and yellow (C)
- Size 6 (4.25mm) straight needles
- Size 8 (5mm) 24-inch circular needles or size needed to obtain gauge
- Stitch holder
- 2 split stitch markers
- Yarn needle

Gauge

21 sts = 4 inches/10cm in Slip St pat on larger needles.
To save time, take time to check gauge.

Special Abbreviation

Make 1 (M1): Insert tip of LH needle from front to back under horizontal thread between st just worked and next st, k1-tbl.

Pattern Stitch

Slip-Stitch Pattern
Rows 1 and 2: With A, knit across.
Row 3 (RS): With B, K1, *sl 1p, k1; rep from * across.
Row 4: K1, *sl 1p, k1; rep from * across.
Rows 5 and 6: With C, knit across.

Rows 7 and 8: With A, k1, *sl 1p, k1; rep from * across.
Rows 9 and 10: With B, knit across.
Rows 11 and 12: With C, k1, *sl 1p, k1; rep from * across.
Rep Rows 1–12 for pat.

Pattern Notes

Circular needle used to accommodate stitches. Do not join, work back and forth in rows.

Slip stitches purlwise with yarn held on wrong side of work.

When changing colors, drop yarn at end of row; do not cut. Pick up again when needed.

Work increases one stitch in from the edge.

Back

With larger needles and A, cast on 29 (29, 49, 69) sts.

Row 1 (RS): K1, M1, work in Slip-St pat across.

Rep Row 1, inc 1 st by M1 at beg of [every row] until there are 45 (49, 69, 91) sts on needle working inc sts into pat.

Mark each end of last row made for side seams.

Work even in pat as established until piece measures 5 (6, 9, 11) inches from cast-on edge, ending with Row 4, 8 or 12 of pat.

For leg opening: Bind off 5 sts at beg of next 2 rows—35 (39, 59, 81) sts.

Continue in pat until piece measures 7 (8, 12, 15) inches from cast-on edge, ending with Row 4, 8 or 12 of pat.

Neck Band

Row 1 (RS): Work in pat across first 12 (14, 20, 26) sts; place next 11 (11, 19, 29) sts on holder for neck; join 2nd skein of yarn and work in pat across rem 12 (14, 20, 26) sts.

Row 2: Working both sides at once with separate skeins, work in pat across first side; on 2nd side, bind off 2 sts, work in pat across.

Row 3: Work in pat across first side; on 2nd side, bind off 2 sts, work in pat across—10 (12, 18, 24) sts on each side.

Rows 4–6: Work in pat across each side.

Row 7: Work in pat across first side to last 2 sts, k2tog; on 2nd side, k2tog, work in pattern across—9 (11, 17, 23) sts on each side.

Continue in pat as established rep [Rows 4–7] 1 (1, 3, 3) time(s)—8 (10, 14, 20) sts on each side.

Work in pat across each side until piece measures 9 (11, 15, 18) inches from cast-on edge.

Bind off all sts.

Collar
With smaller needles and A, with RS of neck band facing, beg at bind-off on one side and ending at bind-off on other side, pick up and knit 21 (23, 25, 28) sts evenly spaced in ends of rows across neck edge to center front holder; knit next 11 (11, 19, 29) sts from holder; pick up and knit 22 (24, 26, 29) sts evenly spaced in ends of rows across to bind-off—54 (58, 70, 86) sts.

House of White Birches, Berne, Indiana 46711   DRGnetwork.com

Row 1: P2, *k2, p2; rep from * across.

Row 2: Knit the knit sts and purl the purl sts across.

Rep Row 2 until collar measures 4 (4¼, 4½, 4½) inches.

Bind off loosely in ribbing.

Assembly

With matching colors, sew bind-off sts on first and 2nd side of neck band tog, allowing 1 st at each end for seam. With RS tog, sew ends of rows on collar tog from neck band to point where collar will fold. With WS tog, sew rem ends of rows tog.

Front

On opposite ends of rows on neck band, measure and mark 1 (1½, 2, 3) inches on each side of center front neckband seam.

Hold piece with RS facing, with larger needles and A, pick up and knit 11 (17, 25, 31) sts evenly spaced between markers.

Work in garter st (knit every row) until front measures 2 (2, 3, 4) inches from neck band.

For leg opening: Knit next 2 rows, casting on 5 sts at end of each row—21 (27, 35, 41) sts.

Work in pat until piece measures same as back from leg opening to marked row.

Bind off.

Right Leg Band and Side Seam

With smaller needles and A, with RS of right leg opening facing, beg in first bind-off st on back and ending in last cast-on st on front, pick up and knit 38 (42, 54, 58) sts evenly spaced around entire leg opening.

Row 1: P2, *k2, p2; rep from * across.

Row 2: Knit the knit sts and purl the purl sts.

Rep Row 2 until leg band measures 1 (1, 1½, 1½) inches.

Bind off loosely in ribbing; cut yarn leaving end for sewing.

Allowing 1 st at each end of leg band for seam, with RS tog, sew ends of rows on leg band tog, matching bind-off on front to marked row on back. Sew ends of rows on front and back tog on side.

Bottom Band

With smaller needles and A, with RS facing, pick up and knit 82 (86, 126, 158) sts evenly spaced around cast-on and bind-off edges of back and front.

Row 1: P2, *k2, p2; rep from * across.

Row 2: Knit the knit sts and purl the purl sts.

Rep Row 2 until bottom band measures 3 inches.

Bind off loosely.

Left Leg Band and Side Seam

Beg in last cast-on st on front and ending in first bound-off st on back, work same as for right leg band. Sew side seam. Sew ends of bottom band rows tog. ❖

Snowflakes & Trees Dog Sweater

Design by Laura Polley

Skill Level

■■■◻ INTERMEDIATE

Sizes

Small (medium, large, extra-large) Instructions are given for the smallest size, with larger sizes in parentheses. When only 1 number is given, it applies to all sizes. To determine size see General Information on page 3.

Finished Measurements

Chest: 13 (16, 20, 25) inches
Back length: 13 (14, 16, 18) inches (excluding fringe)

Materials

- Worsted yarn: 3½ (4, 6, 7) oz red (A); 3½ oz each green (B), white (C) and variegated (D)
- Size 7 (4.5mm) knitting needles
- Size 9 (5.25mm) 24-inch circular needle
- Size H/8 (5mm) crochet hook
- Stitch holder
- Stitch markers
- Yarn needle
- 1 x 1½ inch cow bell

Gauge

16 sts = 4 inches/10cm in St st.
To save time, take time to check gauge.

Special Abbreviations

Make 1 (M1): Insert tip of LH needle from front to back under horizontal thread between st just worked and next st, k1-tbl.

Decrease (dec): Maintaining color pat, work k2tog on RS row or p2tog on WS row.

Pattern Note

Circular needles used to accommodate stitches. Do not join; work back and forth in rows.

When working from chart all odd-numbered rows are right side rows and are worked from right to left; all even-numbered rows are wrong side rows and are worked from left to right. Make 1 increase is worked one stitch in from each edge.

Back

With larger needles and B, cast on 20 (22, 34, 48) sts.

Rows 1 (RS) and 2: Knit for garter st ridge.

Row 3 (inc row): With A, k1, M1, knit to last st, M1, k1—22 (24, 36, 50) sts.

Beg with Row 4, follow Snowflakes Chart on page 19 through Row 33 (37, 37, 37)—32 (38, 50, 64) sts.

For small and medium sizes only: Cut D. Mark each end of last row for Bottom Band.

For large and extra large sizes only: With D, work in St st until piece measures 7½ (8) inches from cast-on edge. Cut D. Mark each end of last row for bottom band.

Body

Row 1 (RS): With B, for front, cast 20 (26, 30, 36) sts onto same needle as back; knit across cast-on sts and last row on back—52 (64, 80, 100) sts.

Row 2: Knit across.

Row 3: With A, k23 (32, 36, 42), place marker, k26 (26, 39, 52), place marker, k3 (6, 5, 6).

Beg with Row 4, complete Tree Chart on page 18, changing colors between markers as indicated.

With B, knit 2 rows.

With D, beg with knit row, work in St st until piece measures 10 [11, 12½, 15] inches from cast-on at beg of back, ending with WS row.

Shoulders Shaping

Row 1 (RS): Bind off 5 (6, 6, 7) sts (1 loop rem on needle after bind off); knit next 9 (13, 17, 21) sts across front and place on holder; bind off 10 (12, 12, 14) sts; knit last 26 (31, 43, 56) sts across back—27 (32, 44, 57) sts.

Row 2: Bind off 5 (6, 6, 7) sts, purl across back—22 (26, 38, 50) sts.

Work in St st until piece measures 11 (12, 14, 16) inches from cast-on at beg of back, ending with WS row.

With B, knit 2 rows.

Neck Band

Row 1: On first side, with A, knit first 8 (9, 13, 17) sts; for neck, join 2nd skein A, bind off next 6 (8, 12, 16) sts; on 2nd side, knit rem sts—8 (9, 13, 17) sts on each side.

Rows 2–7 (5, 5, 9): Working both sides at once with separate skeins, work in St st across first side to last 2 sts, dec; on 2nd side, work in St st across—5 (7, 11, 13) sts on each side.

Work in St st across each side until piece measures 15 (17, 19, 23) inches from beg cast-on, ending with WS row.

With B, knit 2 rows.

Bind off each side.

Collar

With smaller needles and B, with RS of neck edge facing, beg at front bind-off on one side, pick up and knit 16 (18, 20, 22) sts evenly spaced across ends of rows to neck bind-off at center back, pick up and knit in 6 (8, 12, 16) bind-off sts, pick up and knit 16 (18, 20, 22) sts evenly spaced across ends of rows to front bind-off—38 (44, 52, 60) sts.

Knit 3 rows.

Bind off loosely.

On opposite ends of rows on neck band measure and mark 1 (1½, 2, 2½) inch(es) from center bind-off on each side.

Front

Place 9 (13, 17, 21) sts from holder on larger needle.

With D, work in St st until D section on front measures same as D section on back, ending with WS row.

With B, knit 2 rows.

With A, beg with knit row, work in St st until front measures 12½ (14½, 17, 19) inches from cast-on at beg of back.

Bind off.

Bottom Band

With smaller needles and B, with RS facing, beg in marked row at side of back, *skipping every 5th or 6th row as needed for edge to lay flat, pick up and knit in ends of rows across to cast-on* at beg of back, pick up and knit in each cast-on st on back; rep from * to * across to front cast-on, pick up and knit in each cast-on st on front.

Knit 3 rows.

Bind off loosely.

House of White Birches, Berne, Indiana 46711   DRGnetwork.com

Side Seam

With RS tog and matching leg openings, colors and ends of rows on front and back, and allowing 1 st on each end for seam, sew body rows tog along side.

Right Leg Band

With smaller needles and B, with RS of right leg opening facing, beg in bind-off row on front and ending in marked row on neck band, pick up and knit 36 (44, 50, 54) sts evenly spaced around entire leg opening.

Knit 3 rows.

Bind off loosely.

Left Leg Band

Beg in marked row on neck band and ending in bind-off row on front, work same as right leg band.

Finishing

With B, sew bind-off sts on neck band sides tog. Sew ends of rows on collar tog. With A, sew bind-off sts of front to neck band between markers. With B, sew ends of rows on right leg band tog; rep on left leg band.

For each knot, cut 3-inch strands of D. Holding 4 strands tog as one, fold in half; insert crochet hook from wrong to right side through st, pull fold through st, place yarn ends through fold, pull to tighten. Make additional knots 1 inch apart, place fringe along back edge of bottom band and across seam between neck band and front. There is no fringe on front edge.

Sew cow bell to center of seam between neck band and front. ❖

TREES KEY
■ With A, k on RS, p on WS
☒ With B, k on RS, p on WS

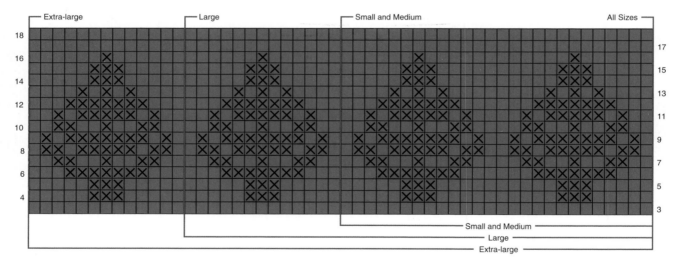

Trees Chart

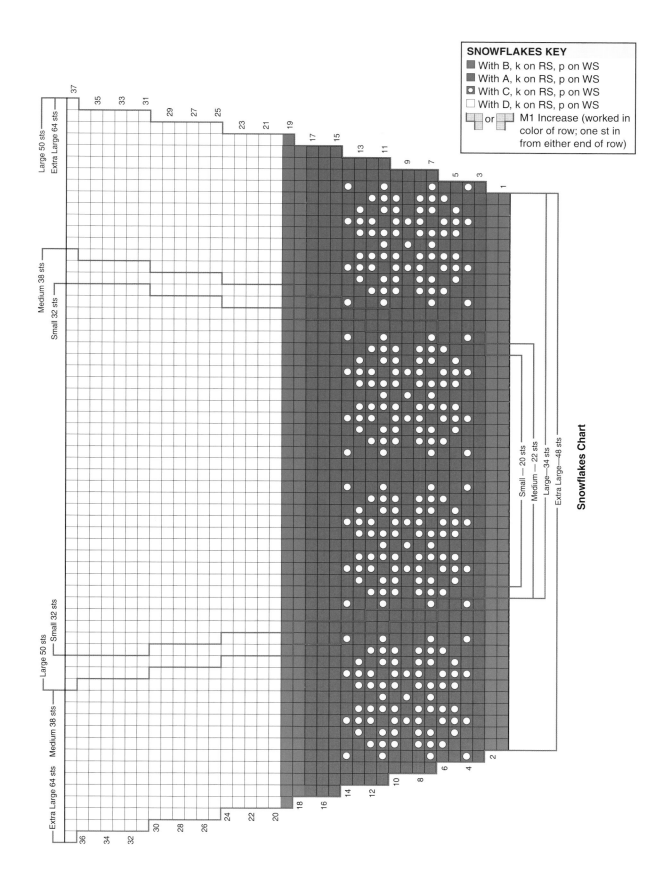

SNOWFLAKES KEY

- ■ With B, k on RS, p on WS
- ■ With A, k on RS, p on WS
- ◙ With C, k on RS, p on WS
- ☐ With D, k on RS, p on WS
- ▨ or ▨ M1 Increase (worked in color of row; one st in from either end of row)

Snowflakes Chart

Small — 20 sts
Medium — 22 sts
Large — 34 sts
Extra Large — 48 sts

Moss & Cables Dog Sweater

Design by Laura Polley

Skill Level

■■■□ INTERMEDIATE

Sizes

Small (medium, large, extra-large) Instructions are given for smallest size, with larger sizes in parentheses. When only 1 number is given, it applies to all sizes. To determine size see General Information on page 3.

Finished Measurements

Chest: 14 (17, 20, 27) inches
Back: 11 (13, 16½, 19½) inches long

Materials

- Worsted weight acrylic/wool blend yarn: 7 (9, 10½, 14) oz off-white
- Size 9 (5.25mm) knitting needles
- Size 10 (5.75mm) 24-inch circular needle or size needed to obtain gauge
- Cable needle
- Stitch holder
- Stitch markers
- Sewing needle and thread
- Yarn needle
- 4 (5, 8, 10) ¾-inch flat buttons

Gauge

16 sts = 4/10 cm in Moss st on larger needles.
50 sts of Center Panel = 7 inches across.
To save time, take time to check gauge.

Special Abbreviations

Increase (inc): Increase 1 st by knitting in front and back of next st.
Decrease (dec): Maintaining pat, work k2tog on RS row or p2tog on WS row.
Cable 4 Front (C4F): Slip next 2 sts to cable needle and hold at front of work, k2, k2 from cable needle.
Cable 4 Back (C4B): Slip next 2 sts to cable needle and hold at back of work, k2, k2 from cable needle.

Cable 6 Front (C6F): Slip next 3 sts to cable needle and hold at front of work, k3, k3 from cable needle.
Cable 6 Back (C6B): Slip next 3 sts to cable needle and hold at back of work, k3, k3 from cable needle.
Twist 3 Front (T3F): Slip next 2 sts to cable needle and hold at front of work, p1, k2 from cable needle.
Twist 3 Back (T3B): Slip next st to cable needle and hold at back of work, k2, p1 from cable needle.

Pattern Stitches

Open Braid (work over center 16 sts)
Row 1 (RS): P2, C4F, p4, C4B, p2.
Row 2: K2, p4, k4, p4, k2.
Row 3: P2, k2, T3F, p2, T3B, k2, p2.
Row 4: K2, p2, k1, p2, k2, p2, k1, p2, k2.
Row 5: P2, k2, p1, T3F, T3B, p1, k2, p2.
Row 6: K2, p2, k2, p4, k2, p2, k2.
Row 7: P2, k2, p2, C4B, p2, k2, p2.
Row 8: K2, p2, k2, p4, k2, p2, k2.
Row 9: P2, k2, p1, T3B, T3F, p1, k2, p2.
Row 10: K2, p2, k1, p2, k2, p2, k1, p2, k2.
Row 11: P2, k2, T3B, p2, T3F, k2, p2.
Row 12: K2, p4, k4, p4, k2.
Rep Rows 1–12 for pat.

Closed Braid (work over 17 sts on each side of Open Braid)
Row 1 (RS): K2, p2, k9, p2, k2.
Row 2: P2, k2, p9, k2, p2.
Row 3: K2, p2, C6F, k3, p2, k2.
Row 4: P2, k2, p9, k2, p2.
Row 5: K2, p2, k9, p2, k2.
Row 6: P2, k2, p9, k2, p2.
Row 7: K2, p2, k3, C6B, p2, k2.
Row 8: P2, k2, p9, k2, p2.
Rep Rows 1–8 for pat.

Moss Stitch
Row 1 (RS): (K1, p1) across designated number of sts, ending with either knit or purl st.
Row 2: Knit the knit sts and purl the purl sts.

Row 3: Purl the knit sts and knit the purl sts.
Row 4: Knit the knit sts and purl the purl sts.
Row 5: Knit the purl sts and purl the knit sts.
Rep Rows 2–5 for pat.

Pattern Note
Circular needle used to accommodate stitches.
Do not join, work back and forth in rows.

Back
With larger needles, cast on 56 (56, 60, 80) sts.

Row 1 (RS): Work Row 1 of Moss St over first 3
(3, 5, 15) sts, place marker for beg of Center Panel;
work Row 1 of Closed Braid pat, work Row 1 of
Open Braid pat, work Row 1 of Closed Braid pat,
place marker for end of Center Panel; work Row 1
of Moss St over last 3 (3, 5, 15) sts.

*Note: 50 sts between markers form center panel.
Work added sts on each side of center panel into
Moss St pat.*

Row 2 (inc row): Inc, work in pat as established
to last st, inc—58 (58, 62, 82) sts.

Rows 3–7 (5, 5, 5): Work even in pat.

Rep [Rows 2–7 (5, 5, 5)] 1 (5, 9, 9) times—60
(68, 80, 100) sts.

Work even in pat until piece measures 3 (4, 5, 6) inches from cast-on edge, ending with WS row.

Body

Row 1 (RS): Work in pat across; for front, cast on 6 (8, 8, 12) sts—66 (76, 88, 112) sts.

Row 2: Work in pat across; for front, cast on 6 (8, 12) sts—72 (84, 96, 124) sts.

Row 3: Work in pat across.

Work in pat until piece measures 6 (8, 10, 13) inches from cast-on edge, ending with WS row.

Next row: For first front, work in pat across first 4 (6, 8, 10) sts; for leg opening, with separate skein, bind off 8 (10, 11, 12) sts (1 loop rem on needle after bind-off); for back, work in pat across next 47 (51, 57, 79) sts; for leg opening, with separate skein, bind off 8 (10, 11, 12); for 2nd front, work in pat across last 3 (5, 7, 9) sts.

Working each section with separate skeins, work in pat until piece measures 7½ (9½, 12½, 15½) inches from cast-on edge, ending with WS row.

Bind off first front; work in pat across back; bind off 2nd front—48 (52, 58, 80) sts.

Neck band

Row 1: For first side, work in pat across first 15 (17, 19, 25) sts, place next 18 (18, 20, 30) sts on holder for neck; for 2nd side, with separate skein, work in pat across last 15 (17, 19, 25) sts.

Row 2: Working both sides at once with separate skeins, work in pat across first side; on 2nd side, bind off 2 (2, 2, 4) sts, work in pat across.

Rows 3–5: Work in pat across first side; on 2nd side, bind off 2 (2, 2, 4) sts, work in pat across—11 (13, 15, 17) sts on each side.

Row 6: Work in pat across first side to last 2 sts, dec; on 2nd side, dec, work in pat across.

Rows 7–9: Rep Row 6—7 (9, 11, 13) sts on each side.

Work in Moss St pat across each side until piece measures 2½ (3, 4, 4½) inches from neck edge holder.

Bind off both sides.

On each side, mark end of row on leg opening edge 1 (1½, 2, 2½) inches from center front bind-off.

Collar

With smaller needles and RS of neck edge facing, beg at bind-off on one side and ending at bind-off on other side, pick up and knit 16 (18, 21, 24) sts evenly spaced in ends of rows across neck edge to sts on holder, knit next 18 (18, 20, 30) sts from holder, pick up and knit 16 (18, 21, 24) sts evenly spaced in ends of rows across to bind-off—50 (54, 62, 78) sts.

Row 1: K2, *p2, k2; rep from * across.

Row 2: Knit the knit sts and purl the purl sts for ribbing.

Rep Row 2 until collar measures 3 (3, 4, 4) inches.

Bind off very loosely in ribbing.

Fold collar to WS and sew bind-off sts to edge where sts are picked up. On each end of collar, flatten collar and sew ends of rows tog from neck edge to fold.

Right leg band

With smaller needles and RS of right leg opening facing, beg in bind-off row on front and ending at marked row on back, pick up and knit 30 (38, 42, 50) sts evenly spaced around entire leg opening.

Row 1: P2, *k2, p2; rep from * across.

Row 2: Knit the knit sts and purl the purl sts for ribbing.

Rep Row 2 until leg band measures 2 (2, 2½, 2½) inches.

Bind off loosely in ribbing; cut yarn leaving end for sewing.

Allowing 1 st at each end of leg band for seam, with RS tog, sew ends of rows on leg band. Sew right front bind-off sts to rem rows on neck band.

Left leg band

Beg in marked row on back and ending in bind-off row on front, work same as right leg band. Sew left front to neck band.

Bottom Band

With smaller needles and RS facing, pick up and knit in 6 (8, 8, 12) cast-on sts at beg of left side of body; skipping every 5th or 6th row so edge will lay flat, pick up and knit in ends of rows across to

back cast-on; pick up and knit in each cast-on st on back; skipping every 5th or 6th row so edge will lay flat, pick up and knit in ends of rows across to body cast-on; pick up and knit in 6 (8, 8, 12) cast-on sts on body; adjust as necessary so that total number of sts is divisible by 4 + 2 sts.

Row 1: P2, *k2, p2; rep from * across.

Row 2: Knit the knits and purl the purls for ribbing.

Rep Row 2 until bottom band measures 2 inches, ending with WS row.

Bind off loosely in ribbing; do not cut yarn.

Button Placket

Continuing in ends of rows on right front and spacing sts evenly, pick up and knit 42 (54, 62, 78) sts in ends of rows up to fold of collar.

Row 1: P2, *k2, p2 rep from * across.

Row 2: Knit the knits and purl the purls for ribbing.

Rows 3–7: Rep Row 2.

Bind off loosely in ribbing.

Buttonhole Placket

With smaller needles, working in ends of rows on left front, beg at fold of collar and spacing sts evenly, pick up and knit 42 (54, 62, 78) sts in ends of rows to bind-off of bottom band.

Row 1: P2, *k2, p2; rep from * across.

Row 2: Knit the knits and purl the purls for ribbing.

Row 3: Rep Row 2.

Row 4 (buttonhole row): K2, *yo, p2tog, rib 10 (10, 6, 6) sts; rep from * across to last 4 sts, yo, p2tog, k2—4 (5, 8, 10) buttonholes.

Row 5: P2, *k2, p2; rep from * across.

Rows 6 and 7: Rep Row 2.

Bind off loosely in ribbing.

Sew buttons on button placket opposite button-holes on buttonhole placket. ❖

House of White Birches, Berne, Indiana 46711   DRGnetwork.com

Stripes Dog Sweater

Design by Laura Polley

Skill Level

 INTERMEDIATE

Sizes

Small (medium, large, extra-large) Instructions are given for smallest size with larger sizes in parentheses. When only 1 number is given it applies to all sizes. To determine size see General Information on page 3.

Finished Measurements

Chest: 13¾ (16, 19, 24) inches
Back: 10 (12, 15½, 18½) inches long

Materials

- Worsted weight yarn: 3½ (3½, 6, 6) oz off-white (A); 3½ oz aqua (B); 1½ oz each pink (C), tan (D) and teal (E)
- Size 7 (4.5mm) needles
- Size 8 (5.0mm) 24-inch circular needle or size needed to obtain gauge
- Yarn needle
- 6 (6, 6, 8) ⅝-inch flat buttons

Gauge

18 sts and 24 rows = 4 inches/10cm in St st on larger needles.
To save time, take time to check gauge.

Special Abbreviations

Decrease (dec): Maintaining color pat, work k2tog on RS row or p2tog on WS row.
Increase (inc): Maintaining color pat inc 1 st by knitting in front and back of next st.

Stripe Sequence

Work in St st in following color sequence:
*2 rows A,
2 rows C,
2 rows A,
2 rows D,
2 rows A,
2 rows B,
2 rows A,
2 rows E.
Rep from * for pat.

Pattern Note

Circular needle used to accommodate stitches. Do not join, work back and forth in rows.

Body

With larger needle and A, beg at right center front and working around Body, cast on 30 (41, 47, 61) sts.

Row 1 (WS): Beg with purl row, work in Stripe Sequence.

Row 2 (RS): K1, dec, work in pat to last 3 sts, dec, k1—28 (39, 45, 59) sts.

Row 3: Work in pat across.

Rep [Rows 2 and 3] 1 (3, 4, 7) times—26 (33, 37, 45) sts.

Work 2 rows even in pat.

For leg opening: Bind off 11 (16, 16, 16) sts, work in pat across—15 (17, 21, 29) sts.

Work 5 rows even in pat, ending last row at leg opening edge.

Right Back

Row 1 (RS): Work in pat across, cast on 5 sts at tail edge—20 (22, 26, 34) sts.

Row 2: Work in pat across.

Rows 3–5: Rep [Rows 1 and 2] twice—30 (32, 36, 44) sts.

Row 6: Work in pat across, cast on 11 (16, 16, 16) sts for back of leg opening—41 (48, 52, 60) sts.

Row 7: Work in pat across, cast on 5 sts at tail edge—46 (53, 57, 65) sts.

Row 8: Work in pat across.

Row 9: Beg at neck edge, inc, work in pat across, cast on 2 (4, 6, 5) sts at tail edge—49 (58, 64, 71) sts.

For small and medium sizes only: Work in pat inc at neck edge [every row] 4 (6) times—53 (64) sts.

Next row: Work in pat ending at neck edge.

For large and extra-large only: Work in pat inc at neck edge [every row] twice.
At end of last row, cast on 5 sts—71 (78) sts.

Work in pat inc at neck edge [every row] twice.
At end of last row, cast on 2 sts—75 (82) sts.

Work in pat inc at neck edge [every row] 4 (11) times—79 (93) sts.

Work 3 (2) rows in pat, ending last row at neck edge.

Neck shaping
Row 1 (RS): Bind off 10 sts, work in pat across—43 (54, 69, 83) sts. Mark first st for neck edge.

Row 2: Work in pat across.

Row 3: Bind off 2 sts, work in pat across—41 (52, 67, 81) sts.

Rep [Rows 2 and 3] 1 (2, 2, 2) times—39 (48, 63, 77) sts.

Work 12 (12, 18, 24) rows even in pat.

Next row: Work in pat across, cast on 2 sts at neck edge—41 (50, 65, 79) sts.

Next row: Work in pat across.

Rep [last 2 rows] 1 (2, 2, 2) times—43 (54, 69, 83) sts)

Next row: Work in pat across, cast on 10 sts at end of row—53 (64, 79, 93) sts. Mark last st for neck edge.

Work 2 rows even in pat.

Shoulder shaping

Row 1 (RS): K1, dec, work in pat across—52 (63, 78, 92) sts.

Row 2: Work in pat across to last 3 sts, dec, p1—51 (62, 77, 91) sts.

Row 3: K1, dec, work in pat across—50 (61, 76, 90) sts.

For sizes medium, large and extra-large only:
Rep [Rows 2 and 3] 1 (1, 4) times—59 (74, 82) sts.

For all sizes:
Next row: Bind off 3 (3, 2, 2) at tail edge, work in pat to last 3 sts, dec, p1—46 (55, 71, 79) sts).

Next row: K1, dec, work in pat across—45 (54, 70, 78) sts.

For large and extra-large only:
Next row: Bind off 5 sts, work in pat across to last 3 sts, dec, p1—64 (72) sts.

Next row: K1, dec, work in pat across—63 (71) sts.

For extra-large size only:
Next row: Bind off 5 sts, work in pat across to last 3 sts, dec, p1—65 sts.

Next row: Work in pat across.

For all sizes:
Next row: Bind off 5 sts, work in pat across—40 (49, 58, 60) sts.

For large size only:
Next row: Work in pat across.

Next row: Bind off 5 sts, work in pat across—53 sts.

For all sizes:
Next row: For back of leg opening, bind off 11 (16, 16, 16) at neck edge, work in pat across—29 (33, 37, 44) sts.

Next row: Bind off 5 sts at tail edge, work in pat across—24 (28, 32, 39) sts.

Next row: Work in pat across.

Rep [last 2 rows] twice—14 (18, 22, 29) sts.

Work 6 (4, 4, 4) rows even in pat, ending last row at tail edge.

Front
Row 1 (WS): Work in pat across; for front of leg opening, cast on 11 (16, 16, 16) sts, ending at shoulder edge—25 (34, 38, 45) sts.

Row 2: Work in pat across.

Row 3: For shoulder shaping, work in pat across to last st, inc—26 (35, 39, 46) sts.

Row 4: Inc, work in pat across—27 (36, 40, 47) sts.

Rep [Rows 3 and 4] 1 (2, 3, 7) times—29 (40, 46, 61) sts.

For sizes small, medium and large only: Rep [Row 3] once—30 (41, 47) sts.

For all sizes: Work 1 (3, 3, 2) rows even in pat.

Bind off.

Neck band
With smaller needles and B, with RS of back neck edge facing, beg and ending in marked sts and working in sts and in ends of rows, pick up and knit 40 (44, 52, 60) sts evenly spaced across neck edge.

Knit 5 rows.

Bind off loosely.

Right leg band
With smaller needles and B, with RS of right leg opening facing, beg in first bind-off st on front and ending in last cast-on st on back, pick up and knit 38 (40, 40, 40) sts evenly spaced around entire leg opening.

Knit 5 rows.

Bind off loosely; cut yarn leaving end for sewing.

For shoulder seam, allowing 1 st at each end for seam, with RS tog, sew ends of rows on leg band together. Sew ends of rows on front and back tog along diagonal shoulder edge.

Left leg band

Beg in first bind-off st on back and ending in last cast-on st on front, work same as for right leg band. Sew shoulder seam.

Bottom band

On opposite ends of rows from neck band, with RS facing, using smaller needles and B, beg in bind-off row on left front, pick up and knit 5 sts across ends of every 6 rows and pick up and knit in each st across to cast-on row on right front.

Next 5 rows: Knit to first corner at tail edge, inc, knit to next corner, inc, knit across.

Bind off.

Button Placket

With smaller needles and B, with RS facing, working in ends of rows on bottom band and neck band and in cast-on sts and spacing sts evenly, pick up and knit 36 (46, 53, 64) sts across right front edge.

Knit 5 rows.

Bind off loosely.

Buttonhole Placket

With smaller needles and B, with RS facing, working in ends of rows on neck band, bottom band and in bind-off sts and spacing sts evenly, pick up and knit 36 (46, 53, 64) sts across left front edge.

Knit 2 rows.

Next row (buttonhole row): K2 (2, 3, 3), *yo, k2tog, k4 (6, 7, 6); rep from * 4 (4, 4, 6) times, yo, k2tog, k2 (2, 3, 3)—6 (6, 6, 8) buttonholes.

Knit 2 rows.

Bind off loosely.

Sew buttons on button placket opposite buttonholes on buttonhole placket. ❖

My Dog & Me

Designs by Bonnie Franz

Skill Level

 INTERMEDIATE

Sizes

Adult sweater: Extra-small (small, medium, large, extra-large, 2X-large) Instructions are given for smallest size, with larger sizes in parentheses. When only 1 number is given, it applies to all sizes.
Dog sweater: Medium To determine size see General Information on page 3.

Finished Measurements

Adult Sweater
Chest: 32 (36½, 40, 43½, 48, 51½) inches
Length: 23 (24, 25, 26½, 27½, 28½) inches
Sleeve length: 16½ (17½, 17½, 18, 18½, 19½) inches

Dog Sweater
Chest: 17½ inches
Back: 14 inches long

Materials
- Bulky weight yarn: 25 (25, 28, 32, 35, 39) oz dark purple (MC); 7 (7, 10½, 10½, 14, 14) oz red (CC)
- Size 9 (5.5mm) 16-inch circular and double-pointed needles
- Size 10½ (6.5mm) 16-, 24- and 36-inch circular and double-pointed needles or size needed to obtain gauge
- Stitch markers
- Stitch holders
- 1 toggle button

Blocked Gauge

14 sts and 21 rows = 4 inches/10cm in St st with larger needles.
To save time, take time to check gauge.

Stripe Sequence
Work following color sequence in St st
6 rnds/rows MC
1 rnd/row CC
1 rnd/row MC
1 rnd/row CC
Rep these 9 rnds/rows for pat.

Pattern Notes
Pullover is worked in the round on circular needles to the underarm. Upper portion is worked back and forth in rows. Sleeves are worked on double-pointed and circular needles in the round.

Dog sweater may be made larger by adding 4 stitches for every added 1 inch of body girth. Add extra length after body band.

Yarn amounts sufficient for both pullover and dog sweater.

Adult Sweater

Body
With MC and smaller circular needle, cast on 50 (58, 62, 68, 76, 80) sts, place marker, cast on 50 (58, 62, 68, 76, 80) sts.

Join without twisting, place marker between first and last st.

Work in k1, p1 rib for 2 inches, inc 12 (12, 16, 16, 16, 20) sts evenly on last rnd—112 (128, 140, 152, 168, 180) sts.

Change to larger needles.

Work even in Stripe Sequence until body measures 14 (14½, 15, 15½, 16, 16) inches.

Divide for front and back
K56 (64, 70, 76, 84, 90) sts and place on holder for front, knit to end of row.

Back
Work in rows in established color sequence until armhole measures 9 (9½, 10, 11, 11½, 12½) inches.

Bind off all sts.

Front
Sl sts from holder to needle.

Work as for back until armhole measures 6 (6½, 7, 8, 8, 9) inches, ending with a WS row.

Shape neck
Next row: K22 (25, 28, 30, 34, 37) sts, place center 12 (14, 14, 16, 16, 16) sts on holder, join 2nd ball of yarn and k22 (25, 28, 30, 34, 37) sts.

Working on both sides of neck with separate skeins, dec 1 st at each neck edge [every other row] 4 (4, 5, 5, 5, 6) times—18 (21, 23, 25, 29, 31) sts.

Work even until armhole measures same as back.

Bind off all sts.

Sleeves
Using MC and dpn, cast on 24 (26, 30, 32, 32, 36) sts.

Join without twisting, place marker between first and last st.

Work even in k1, p1 rib for 2 inches, inc 2 (2, 2, 2, 4, 4) sts evenly on last rnd—26 (28, 32, 34, 36, 40) sts.

Change to larger needles.

Working in Stripe Sequence, inc 1 st each side of marker [every 3rd rnd] 12 (12, 8, 18, 16, 16) times, then [every 4th round] 5 (6, 9, 2, 4, 5) times—60, (64, 66, 74, 76, 82) sts.

Change to longer circular needles as necessary.

Work even until sleeve measures 16½ (17½, 17½, 18, 18½, 19½) inches. Bind off all sts.

Sew shoulder seams.

Neck Band
With MC and smaller circular needle, pick up and knit 58 (62, 64, 68, 72, 74) sts around neck edge including sts on holder.

Join, place marker between first and last st.

Work in k1, p1 rib for 6 rnds.

Bind off loosely in pat.

Assembly
Sew sleeves into armholes.

Dog Sweater

Body
Beg at tail, with MC and smaller needles, cast on 46 sts.

Work even in k1, p1 rib for 6 rows.

Change to larger needles.

Work Stripe Sequence in rows until body measures 6 inches, ending with a RS row.

Cast on 15 sts at end of last row—61 sts.

Stomach band
Join, place marker between first and last st.

Work in rnds until band measures 3 inches, ending 15 sts before marker on last rnd.

Next row: Bind off 15 sts, remove marker work to end of row.

Work even in rows from this point until sweater measures 13 inches.

Change to smaller needles.

With MC only, work even in k1, p1 rib for 6 rows.

Beg neck strap
Next row: Bind off 40 sts, work to end of row.

Work even in garter st on rem 6 sts until strap measures 6½ inches or desired length.

Buttonhole row: K2, k2tog, yo, k2.

Work even in garter st for additional ½ inch.

Bind off all sts.

Sew button opposite buttonhole. ❖

House of White Birches, Berne, Indiana 46711   DRGnetwork.com

Beauty & Her Beast Leg Warmers

Designs by Kathy Sasser

Skill Level
◼◼☐☐ EASY

Sizes
Girl's small (medium, large)
Dog's small (medium, large) Instructions are given for smallest size, with larger sizes in parentheses. When only 1 number is given, it applies to all sizes.

Finished Measurements

Girl's Warmers
Length: 9½ (10, 11¼) inches
Bottom width: 9 (10, 11) inches
Top width: 10½ (11½, 12½) inches

Dog's Warmers
Length: 4 (7, 9½) inches
Bottom width: 3½ (4½, 5½) inches
Top width: 4½ (6, 7) inches

Materials
- Worsted weight yarn: 4 (4, 8) oz each green (A), pink (B) and dark purple (C)
- Size 5 (3.75mm) needles
- Size 7 (4.5mm) needles or size needed to obtain gauge

Gauge
20 sts and 26 rows = 4 inches/10cm in St st with larger needles.
To save time, take time to check gauge.

Special Abbreviation
Make Bobble (MB): [Purl in front and back of st] twice, purl in front of st again, turn, k5, turn, p5. With LH needle, lift 2nd, 3rd, 4th and 5th sts one at a time over first st and off needle. Push bobble to RS.

Pattern Stitches
1/1 Rib
Row 1 (RS): K1, *p1, k1; rep from * across.
Row 2: P1, *k1, p1; rep from * across.
Rep Rows 1 and 2 for pat.

Color Stripes
Rows 1, 3, 5 and 7 (RS): With C, knit.
Rows 2 and 6: With C, purl.
Row 4 (girl's warmer): With B, p3 (5, 2), *MB, p5; rep from *, end last rep, p3 (5, 2).
Row 4 (dog's warmer): With B, p1 (5, 3), *MB, p5; rep from *, end last rep, p1 (5, 3)
Row 8: With A, purl.
Row 9: With A, knit.
Row 10: With A, purl.
Rep Rows 1–10 for pat.

Pattern Notes
Yarn amounts given are enough to complete a pair of warmers for girl and a pair of warmers for dog.

Girl's leg warmers are designed to fit over pant legs for the following age groups: 4–5 years (6–7 years, 8–9 years).

Bobbles are made on wrong side rows.

Girl's Leg Warmers

Beg at bottom with smaller needles and A, cast on 45 (51, 55) sts.

Work even in 1/1 Rib for 2 inches, inc 10 (9, 10) sts evenly on last WS row—55 (60, 65) sts.

Change to larger needles and St st.

Beg with Row 1 (5, 1), work even in Color Stripe pat for 37 (39, 47) rows.

Change to A and smaller needles.

Next row: Purl, dec 4 (3, 2) sts evenly—
51 (57, 63) sts.

Work even in 1/1 Rib for 2 inches.

Bind off loosely.

Finishing
Sew back seam, matching stripes.

Dog Leg Warmers

Beg at bottom with smaller needles and A, cast on
17 (23, 29) sts.

Work even in 1/1 Rib for ¾ (1, 2) inches, inc 10 (12,
14) sts evenly on last WS row—27 (35, 43) sts.

Change to larger needles and Color Stripe pat.

Work even in pat for 17 (33, 37) rows.

Change to A and smaller needles.

Next row: Purl, dec 4 (4, 6) sts evenly—
23 (31, 37) sts.

Work even in 1/1 Rib for ¾ (1, 2) inches.

Bind off loosely.

Finishing
Sew back seam, matching stripes. ❖

For You & Your Pampered Pooch

Designs by Gayle Bunn

Skill Level

 INTERMEDIATE

Sizes

Hat and Mittens: One size fits most
Dog coat: Extra-small (small, medium, large)
Instructions are given for smallest size, with larger sizes in parentheses. When only 1 number is given, it applies to all sizes. To determine size see General Information on page 3.

Finished Measurements

Mitten
Length: 11 inches

Dog Coat
Chest: 11 (13½, 16, 20) inches
Length: 11 (13, 16, 21) inches

Materials

- Super bulky weight yarn: 14 oz pink (MC)
- Medium weight eyelash-type yarn: 4 oz white (A)
- Bulky weight yarn: 4 oz white (B)
- Size 11 (8mm) straight and double-pointed needles or size needed to obtain gauge
- Size 15 (10mm) straight and 24-inch circular needles or size needed to obtain gauge
- Cable needle
- Stitch holders
- Stitch markers

4 MEDIUM

5 BULKY

6 SUPER BULKY

Gauge

Hat and Dog Coat
6 sts and 12 rows = 4 inches/10cm in St st with MC and larger needles.
Mittens
7 sts and 14 rows = 4 inches/10cm in St st with MC and smaller needles.
To save time, take time to check gauge.

Special Abbreviations

Cable 4 Back (C4B): Sl next 2 sts to cn and hold in back, k2, k2 from cn.
Cable 4 Front (C4F): Sl next 2 sts to cn and hold in front, k2, k2 from cn.
Increase (inc): Increase 1 st by knitting in front and back of next st.

Pattern Stitch

Cable Panel
Row 1 (RS): P1, k8, p1.
Row 2 and all WS rows: K1, p8, k1.
Row 3: P1, C4B, C4F, p1.
Rows 5 and 7: Rep Row 1.
Row 8: Rep Row 2.
Rep Rows 1–8 for pat.

Pattern Notes

Two strands of A and 1 strand of B are held tog for trim. This will be referred to as CC.

Mittens are worked back and forth in rows with a seam at outside of hand.

Hat

With MC and larger needles, cast on 39 sts.

Row 1 (RS): K1, *p1, k1; rep from * across.

Row 2: P1, *k1, p1; rep from * across.

Rep Rows 1 and 2 until hat measures 4 inches, ending with a RS row.

Next row (WS): Rib 15, [inc, rib 3] twice, inc in next st, rib to end of row—42 sts.

Set up pat

Row 1 (RS): Work across first 6 sts and place on holder, k10, place marker, work Row 1 of Cable Panel, place marker, k10, place rem 6 sts on holder.

Row 2: P10, work Row 2 of Cable Panel, p10.

Keeping sts between markers in established Cable Panel and rem sts in St st, work even until hat measures 11 inches from beg, ending with a WS row.

Shape top

Row 1 (RS): Work in pat across 21 sts, turn, leave rem sts unworked.

Row 2: Sl 1p, work in Cable Panel across 10 sts, p2tog, turn, leave rem sts unworked.

Row 3: Sl 1k, work in Cable Panel across 10 sts, ssk, turn, leave rem sts unworked.

Rep Rows 2 and 3 until all sts on either side have been worked.

Place rem 12 sts on holder.

Front edging

With RS facing and MC, work in established rib pat across 6 sts of first holder, pick up and knit 15 sts along side of hat, knit 12 sts from top st holder dec 1 st at center, pick up and knit 16 sts down other side of hat, work in established rib pat across 6 sts of rem st holder—55 sts.

Work even in k1, p1 rib for 3 rows.

Cut MC, change to CC.

Knit 2 rows; purl 1 row.

Loosely bind off knitwise on WS.

Sew neckband seam, including face trim.

Mittens

Left Mitten

With CC and smaller needles, cast on 19 sts loosely.

Row 1 (RS): Purl.

Row 2: Knit.

Row 3: Purl.

Change to MC.

Next row: P3, [inc, p3] twice, inc in next st, purl to end of row—22 sts.

Set up pat

Row 1 (RS): K10, place marker, work Row 1 of Cable Panel, place marker, k2.

Row 2: P2, work Row 2 of Cable Panel, p10.

Keeping sts between markers in established Cable Panel and rem sts in St st, work even until mitten measures 2½ inches from beg, ending with a WS row.

Beg thumb gusset

Row 1 (RS): K7, inc in each of next 2 sts, work pat to end.

Rows 2–4: Work even in St st.

Row 5: K7, inc, k2, inc, work to end.

Rows 6–8: Work even in St st.

Row 9: K7, inc, k4, inc, work to end.

Row 10: Purl.

Beg thumb

Row 1: K15, turn, leave rem sts unworked.

Row 2: Cast on 1 st, p7, turn, leave rem sts unworked.

Row 3: Cast on 1 st, k8—9 sts.

Work 3 rows even in St st.

Shape top of thumb
Row 1 (RS): [K1, k2tog] 3 times—6 sts.

Row 2: Purl.

Row 3: [K2tog] 3 times—3 sts.

Cut yarn, leaving an 8-inch end. Draw yarn through rem sts twice and pull tightly. Sew thumb seam.

Hand
With RS facing, rejoin yarn to sts from RH needle, pick up and knit 2 sts at base of thumb, work in established pat to end of row.

Next row: Work in established pat, purling tog 2 sts picked up at base of thumb—22 sts.

Work even until mitten measures 10 inches from beg, ending with a WS row.

Shape top
Row 1: [K1, k2tog] 7 times, k1—15 sts.

Row 2: Purl.

Row 3: [K2tog] 7 times, k1—8 sts.

Cut yarn leaving a long end. Draw yarn through rem sts twice and pull tightly. Sew side seam.

Right Mitten
With CC and smaller needles, cast on 19 sts loosely.

Row 1 (RS): Purl.

Row 2: Knit.

Row 3: Purl.

Change to MC.

Next row: P10, [inc in next st, p3] twice, inc in next st, purl to end of row—22 sts.

Set up pat
Row 1 (RS): K2, place marker, work Row 1 of Cable Panel, place marker, k10.

Row 2: P10, work Row 2 of Cable Panel, p2.

Keeping sts between markers in established Cable Panel and rem sts in St st, work even until mitten measures 2½ inches from beg, ending with a WS row.

Beg thumb gusset
Row 1: Work in established pat across 12 sts, inc in each of next 2 sts, knit to end of row.

Complete thumb and remainder of mitten as for left mitten.

Dog Coat

Beg at collar with CC and larger needles, loosely cast on 18 (22, 26, 32) sts.

Row 1 (RS): Purl.

Row 2: Knit.

Row 3: Purl.

Change to MC.

Inc row: P6 (8, 10, 13), [inc 1 st in next st, p3] twice, purl to end of row—20 (24, 28, 34) sts.

Set up pat
Row 1 (RS): K5 (7, 9, 12), place marker, work Row 1 of Cable Panel, place marker, k5 (7, 9, 12).

Row 2: P5 (7, 9, 12), work Row 2 of Cable Panel, p5 (6, 9, 12).

Keeping sts between markers in established Cable Panel and rem sts in St st, inc 1 st each end [every RS row] 4 (5, 6, 7) times—28 (34, 40, 48) sts.

Work even until coat measures 3½ (4, 6, 8) inches above collar, ending with a WS row.

Leg openings
Row 1: K3 (5, 7, 9), bind off 3 (4, 4, 5) sts, work in pat across 16 (16, 18, 20) sts, bind off 3 (4, 4, 5) sts, k3 (5, 7, 9).

Note: All leg sections are worked at the same time using a separate ball of yarn for each section.

Beg with a WS row, work even for 3 (5, 5, 7) rows.

Next row (RS): K3 (5, 7, 9), cast on 3 (4, 4, 5) sts, work in pat across 16 (16, 18, 20) sts, cast on 3 (4, 4, 5) sts, k3 (5, 7, 9)—28 (34, 40, 48) sts.

Work even in established pat until coat measures 6 (8, 11, 16) inches above collar, ending with a WS row.

Back shaping
Bind off 3 (4, 5, 7) sts at beg of next 2 rows—22 (26, 30, 34) sts.

Dec row: Ssk, work in pat to last 2 sts, k2tog.

Next row: Work even in pat.

Rep [last 2 rows] 9 (10, 11, 13) times—10 (14, 18, 22) sts.

Work even until back measures 5 inches above bind-off back sts.

Place rem sts on holder; cut MC.

Back edging
With RS facing, using larger circular needle and MC, pick up and knit 11 (14, 19, 25) sts along bound-off and shaped back edge, work across 10 (14, 18, 22) sts from holder dec 2 sts evenly across, pick up and knit 11 (14, 19, 25) sts along opposite side of back—30 (40, 54, 70) sts.

Change to CC.

Knit 1 row; purl 1 row.

Loosely bind off knitwise on WS.

Sew collar and body seam.

Legs
With dpn and MC, pick up and knit 18 (20, 20, 24) sts around leg opening.

Divide sts so there are 6 (8, 8, 8) sts on first needle and 6 (6, 6, 8) sts each on 2nd and 3rd needles. Join, place marker between first and last st.

Work even in k1, p1 ribbing for 3 rnds.

Bind off in rib.

Rep for other leg opening. ❖

Home for the Family Dog

Design by Lois S. Young

Skill Level

 INTERMEDIATE

Finished Sizes
Approx 30 x 31 inches

Materials
- Worsted weight yarn: 12 oz beige (A), 32 oz gray (B)
- Size 7 (4.5 mm) needles or size needed to obtain gauge
- Sharp and blunt point tapestry needles
- Double-bed size extra-loft quilt batting (¾ inch thick)

Gauge
18 sts and 22 rows = 4 inches/10cm in St st.
To save time, take time to check gauge.

Pattern Notes
Slip the first stitch of each row purlwise for a chain selvage.

Sew all seams by holding wrong sides together and overcasting edge through the chain selvage.

Top
With MC, cast on 27 sts.

Referring to Chart, make 25 squares, 12 with A as MC and B as CC, 13 with B as MC and A as CC.

Sew squares tog in checkerboard pat.

Bottom and sides
With B, cast on 135 sts.

Work 16 rows garter st for one side.

Turning row (RS): Purl.

Continue in garter st until piece measures 31 inches, ending on a WS row.

Note: Rows between turning rows form bottom.

Turning row: Purl.

Work 16 rows of garter st for 2nd side.

Bind off knitwise on WS.

Next Side: *With RS facing, pick up and knit 3 sts for every 4 rows along side of bottom.

Work 16 rows garter st.

Bind off knitwise on WS.

Rep from * along 4th side of bottom.

STITCH & COLOR KEY
☐ With MC, K on RS, p on WS
▨ With CC, P on RS, k on WS
⌢ With MC, sl 1 purlwise
⊟ With MC, K on WS

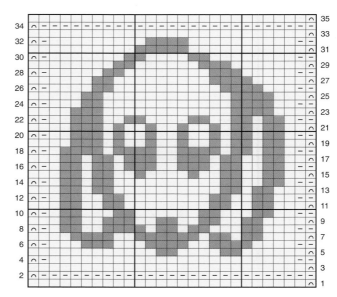

DOG CHART

Assembly

Sew tog edges of sides to make an "open box" shape.

Cut 4 layers of quilt batting to fit square. With sharp needle, loosely tack top to batting at each spot where squares intersect.

Place top and bottom tog and sew edges.

Run in dryer on air fluff setting for 5 minutes to fluff up batting. ❖

House of White Birches, Berne, Indiana 46711   DRGnetwork.com

Best Friend Tote & Vest

Designs by Ellen Edwards Drechsler

Skill Level

■■■□ INTERMEDIATE

Finished Size
Tote Base and Sides: Approx 15 x 62 inches (before felting)
Tote: Approx 8½ x 15 x 9 inches (after felting and assembly, and excluding handles)
Vest circumference: Approx 14 inches
Vest length: Approx 8 inches

Materials
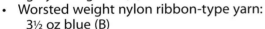
- Worsted weight wool yarn: 21 oz blue/ gray variegated (A)
- Worsted weight nylon ribbon-type yarn: 3½ oz blue (B)
- Size 8 (5mm) straight and 16-inch circular needles
- Size 13 (9mm) 2 double-pointed and 29-inch circular needles or size needed to obtain gauge
- Stitch markers
- Box same size as desired size of tote for shaping after felting
- Sewing needle and matching thread
- Size H/8 (5mm) crochet hook (for fringe)
- Plastic canvas (optional for bottom of tote)

Gauge
11 sts = 4 inches/10cm in St st with larger needles and 2 strands of A (before felting).

20 sts = 4 inches/10cm in St st with smaller needles and B.

Exact gauge is not critical to this project, but stitches should be light and airy before felting.

Pattern Notes
Tote is knitted with 2 strands of A held together throughout.

Yarn amount given for B is sufficient for both tote trim and dog vest.

Tote

Base
With circular needle and 2 strands of A, cast on 30 sts. Work in garter st in rows until there are 50 ridges.

Sides
K30, place marker, pick up and knit 50 sts across long edge of base, place marker, pick up and knit 30 sts across cast-on edge, place marker, pick up and knit 50 sts across rem long edge—160 sts.

Join and work St st in rnds until sides measure 13 inches.

*Purl 1 rnd, knit 1 rnd; rep from * until there are 6 ridges on RS. Bind off all sts.

I-Cord Handles
With dpn and 2 strands of A, cast on 8 sts, *sl sts to other end of needle, pull yarn firmly across back, k8; rep from * until cord measures approx 71 inches. Bind off.

Felting
Place tote and I-cord in a pillowcase or laundry bag. Set the washer to hot wash, cold rinse and lowest water level. Add a small amount of detergent. Add a pair of jeans to help in the agitation process. Check on the piece every 5 minutes. Felting could take 20–25 minutes or so. Keep setting back the timer to make the wash cycle longer. When desired felting is achieved, rinse and spin very lightly. Excessive spinning can set creases. Excess water can also be removed by rolling pieces in a towel.

After felting, place empty plastic bag over appropriate-size box and place box inside tote to shape it. Allow to dry with box inside.

Assembly

Mark 4 corners of bag with straight pins. On top edge of 1 short side, mark a semicircle. Zigzag st by hand, or machine if desired, to reinforce edge. Cut out semicircle.

Binding

With B and smaller needles, cast on 9 sts.

Row 1: K4, p1, k4.

Row 2 (RS): P4, k1, p4.

Rep Rows 1 and 2 until binding measures same as top edge of tote. Bind off.

Pin binding around top edge of tote with knit st along edge; with needle and thread, sew in place on inside and outside edges.

Fringe

For each knot, cut 5-inch strand of B. Fold strand in half. Insert crochet hook from wrong to right side through st and draw folded end through. Pull loose ends through folded section. Draw knot up firmly to tighten. Make additional knots through each knit st at top edge of binding around edge of tote.

Handles

Cut I-cord into 2 pieces of desired length, allowing approx 2 inches on each end to attach handle. Pinch corner edges tog

where pinned. Place 1 end of handle in each corner. Sew securely in place.

Vest

With circular needle, cast on 70 sts. Join without twisting, mark beg of rnd.

Rnds 1–10: *K1, p1; rep from * around.

Rnds 11–14: Work in St st.

Fringe border

Rnd 1: *K6, p1; rep from * around.

Rnd 2: *P1, k4, p1, k1; rep from * around.

Rnd 3: *K1, p1, k2, p1, k2; rep from * around.

Rnd 4: *K2, p2tog, k3; rep from * around—61 sts.

Work 4 rnds even in St st, ending last rnd 12 sts before beg of rnd marker, bind off next 24 sts—37 sts rem.

Slipping first st of every row, work 6 rows even in St st.

Dec row (RS): Sl 1, ssk, knit to last 3 sts, k2tog, k1.

Work in St st, rep dec row [every RS row] 9 more times; dec 1 st in center of last row—16 sts rem.

Edging

With RS facing, place marker after 16 sts on needle, pick up and knit 1 st in each sl st and each st around edge. Join. Beg with a purl rnd, work 5 rnds in garter st. Bind off all sts.

Fringe

For fringe, cut 3-inch strands of B. Work knots same as for tote, pulling 1 strand of fringe through each purl st in Rnds 1–4 of fringe border. ❖

Photo Index

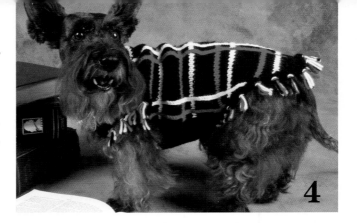

24

20

42

40

32

28

35

Metric Conversion Charts

METRIC CONVERSIONS

yards	x	.9144	=	metres (m)
yards	x	91.44	=	centimetres (cm)
inches	x	2.54	=	centimetres (cm)
inches	x	25.40	=	millimetres (mm)
inches	x	.0254	=	metres (m)

centimetres	x	.3937	=	inches
metres	x	1.0936	=	yards

INCHES INTO MILLIMETRES & CENTIMETRES (Rounded off slightly)

inches	mm	cm	inches	cm	inches	cm	inches	cm
1/8	3	0.3	5	12.5	21	53.5	38	96.5
1/4	6	0.6	5 1/2	14	22	56	39	99
3/8	10	1	6	15	23	58.5	40	101.5
1/2	13	1.3	7	18	24	61	41	104
5/8	15	1.5	8	20.5	25	63.5	42	106.5
3/4	20	2	9	23	26	66	43	109
7/8	22	2.2	10	25.5	27	68.5	44	112
1	25	2.5	11	28	28	71	45	114.5
1 1/4	32	3.2	12	30.5	29	73.5	46	117
1 1/2	38	3.8	13	33	30	76	47	119.5
1 3/4	45	4.5	14	35.5	31	79	48	122
2	50	5	15	38	32	81.5	49	124.5
2 1/2	65	6.5	16	40.5	33	84	50	127
3	75	7.5	17	43	34	86.5		
3 1/2	90	9	18	46	35	89		
4	100	10	19	48.5	36	91.5		
4 1/2	115	11.5	20	51	37	94		

KNITTING NEEDLES CONVERSION CHART

Canada/U.S.	0	1	2	3	4	5	6	7	8	9	10	10½	11	13	15
Metric (mm)	2	2¼	2¾	3¼	3½	3¾	4	4½	5	5½	6	6½	8	9	10

CROCHET HOOKS CONVERSION CHART

Canada/U.S.	1/B	2/C	3/D	4/E	5/F	6/G	8/H	9/I	10/J	10½/K	N
Metric (mm)	2.25	2.75	3.25	3.5	3.75	4.25	5	5.5	6	6.5	9.0

Skill Levels

BEGINNER

Beginner projects for first-time knitters using basic stitches. Minimal shaping.

EASY

Easy projects using basic stitches, repetitive stitch patterns, simple color changes and simple shaping and finishing.

INTERMEDIATE

Intermediate projects with a variety of stitches, mid-level shaping and finishing.

EXPERIENCED

Experienced projects using advanced techniques and stitches, detailed shaping and refined finishing.

E-mail: Customer_Service@whitebirches.com

HOUSE of WHITE BIRCHES
PUBLISHERS SINCE 1947

Pet Pleasers for Dog Lovers is published by DRG, 306 East Parr Road, Berne, IN 46711, telephone (260) 589-4000. Printed in USA. Copyright © 2009 DRG. All rights reserved. This publication may not be reproduced in part or in whole without written permission from the publisher.

RETAIL STORES: If you would like to carry this pattern book or any other DRG publications, call the Wholesale Department at Annie's Attic to set up a direct account: (903) 636-4303. Also, request a complete listing of publications available from DRG.

Every effort has been made to ensure that the instructions in this pattern book are complete and accurate. We cannot, however, take responsibility for human error, typographical mistakes or variations in individual work.

STAFF

Editor: Jeanne Stauffer
Managing Editor: Dianne Schmidt
Technical Editor: Kathy Wesley
Copy Supervisor: Michelle Beck
Copy Editor: Amanda Ladig

Graphic Arts Supervisor: Ronda Bechinski
Graphic Artist: Nicole Gage
Art Director: Brad Snow
Assistant Art Director: Nick Pierce

ISBN: 978-1-59217-253-5

1 2 3 4 5 6 7 8 9